Bailey & Canteen Theme

They ride across the prairie wide,
They're always side by side,
From dawn till setting sun.
You won't see one without the other,
They're closer than brothers,
Bailey and Canteen.

Chorus:
Best friends (best friends),
Bailey and Canteen,
Best friends (best friends)—
They're brown as a berry from ridin' the prairie.
All day long, they sing this song:
"We're joined by the heart, never apart, best friends."

Bridge:
You'll never see Canteen without Bailey by his side;
They started out together and partnered up for life.
Like birds of a feather, they stick together,
Bailey and Canteen.

Except as noted below, all sound tracks and vocals recorded and mixed by Aaron Minick at The Play Room Studio, Smyrna, TN. Mastered by Marty Shrabel at AHA Productions, Goodlettsville, TN. "Bailey & Canteen Theme" audio track recorded and engineered by Mike McIntyre at Wright Studio, Nashville, TN.

Eddy Bolton: Series writer and creator; co-producer of audio tracks and story narrator.
Johnny Minick: Co-producer of audio tracks; voice for introduction.
Aaron Minick: Co-producer of audio tracks; arranged sound effects and background music; audio engineer for vocals.
Mikchael Demus: Audio engineer for music tracks.
Gus Gaches: Co-producer of audio track for "Bailey & Canteen Theme."

Musicians
Harold Bradley: Lead and rhythm guitar. Billy Linneman: Upright bass. Aaron Minick: Drums, percussion, and keyboard. Johnny Minick: Accordion and piano. Bruce Watkins: Fiddle, mandolin, lead and rhythm guitar, and upright bass. Jason Webb: Piano, strings, and keyboard.

Vocalists
Voice of Bailey: Julie Bolton. "Bailey & Canteen Theme" vocals: Eddy Bolton, Aaron Minick, and Johnny Minick. "Bailey & Canteen Theme" children's background vocals: Megan Cannon, Rachel Elrod, Kylie Gaches, Briana Sparks, Megan Watson, Brooke Welch, and Jordan Welch. "With God's Help" background vocals: Sherry Minick, Amanda Williams, Karen Williams, and Lyndsey Williams.

Special thanks to Sandy Brazile and The Bailey Hat Company, Fort Worth, Texas.
Eddy Bolton is an endorsed artist for Greg Bennett Guitars.

ISBN 0-7847-1825-3

12 11 10 09 08 07 06   9 8 7 6 5 4 3 2 1

Lost and Found

STORY & SONGS BY **EDDY BOLTON**

ILLUSTRATED BY **JERRY PITTENGER**

Standard PUBLISHING
Bringing The Word to Life

Cincinnati, Ohio

Bailey came bouncing into the barn,
Gave Canteen a scoop of oats and some hay,
Then raked and shoveled out the other stalls
'Cause Dad said they had to be cleaned today.

Now he could hardly wait to get out on the trail,
But doin' the chores came first.
He remembered God said to obey your parents,
And with God's help it didn't seem like work.

Then he brushed Canteen till his coat sparkled—
Why, he looked too pretty to put the saddle on!

So Bailey decided to ride bareback today
And cool off in the old swimmin' hole.

He'd swing on a rope that was tied to a limb,
Then drop into the water below.
And he loved the way that river mud felt
When it squished up between his toes.

Well, Bailey had no sooner made his first splash
When they heard a strange noise on the wind.

Canteen's ears stood erect, as he turned his neck,
Then they ran for a look round the bend.

There, on a rock in the middle of the stream,
Was a little lost puppy, wet and frail.

But the minute he saw Bailey and Canteen,
He started barking and wagging his tail.

Bailey prayed, "Lord, we sure need your help
To rescue this puppy we found.
'Cause where he's a-settin', if we don't help him,
He could slip into the water and drown."

Right then God showed Bailey just what to do.
He said, "Don't worry, you've got nothing to fear.
Canteen can push that big boulder in the river,
Then you can get over there from here."

Ker-splash! went the boulder as it fell into the river,
Then Bailey jumped from one rock to the next.

And he just got bathed with puppy kisses,
As he hugged the pup up to his chest.

Yep, you guessed it . . .

They named him Lucky, 'cause they were lucky to find him—
Just seemed like the right name to choose.
So now if you get to see Bailey and Canteen,
Lucky will be there too!

Round up all these Bailey & Canteen adventures!

0-7847-1824-5

0-7847-1825-3

0-7847-1826-1

0-7847-1851-2

0-7847-1850-4